CW01455562

IAIN SINCLAIR was born in 1943 in Cardiff, Wales and studied at Trinity College, Dublin, and the Courtauld Institute, London. A renowned essayist and writer of fiction, his early work consisted mostly of poetry, which he published on his own small press, Albion Village Press. He has written and presented a number of films and has co-directed with Chris Petit four documentaries for Channel 4, one of which, *Asylum*, won the short film prize at the Montreal Festival. He was also the editor of the Paladin Poetry Series. His book *Downriver* won the James Tait Black Memorial Prize and the Encore Award, and he has since produced many books including: *Radon Daughters*; *Lights Out for the Territory*; *London Orbital*; *Edge of the Orison*; *London: City of Disappearances*, (ed.); and *Hackney, That Rose-Red Empire: A Confidential Report*. For the Swedenborg Society he has written *Swimming to Heaven: the Lost Rivers of London* (2013) and, with Brian Catling, *Several Clouds Colliding* co-published with BookWorks. His most recent book *Living with Buildings: And Walking with Ghosts* was published in 2018.

BLAKE'S LONDON: THE TOPOGRAPHIC SUBLIME is the first in a series of Swedenborg Society pocket books. Drawing on miscellaneous material and other ephemera from the Swedenborg archives, the aim of the pocket book series is to make available, in printed form, lectures, interviews and other unique items that would otherwise remain unseen by a broader audience.

TITLES IN THE SERIES

Blake's London:
the topographic sublime

Blake's London:
the topographic sublime

IAIN SINCLAIR

The Swedenborg Society
20-21 Bloomsbury Way
London
WC1A 2TH

2018

third printing © 2018, The Swedenborg Society/Iain Sinclair

Series editor: Stephen McNeilly

Typeset at Swedenborg House.
Printed at T J International, Padstow.
Cover and book design © Stephen McNeilly
Transcribed by James Wilson

Published by:
The Swedenborg Society
Swedenborg House
20-21 Bloomsbury Way
London WC1A 2TH

ISBN : 978-0-85448-170-5
British Library Cataloguing-in-Publication Data.
A catalogue record for this book
is available from the British Library.

Contents

Preliminary note

Blake's London: the topographic sublime by
Iain Sinclair is the transcript of a talk given at the
Swedenborg Society on Friday the 2nd of November,
2007. The occasion was a one-day conference entitled *Blake in Contexts,* organized conjointly by
the Swedenborg Society and Goldsmiths College,
University of London. The event took place at the
Society's grade II neoclassical hall and was held in
celebration of the 250th anniversary of Blake's birth.
Other speakers on the day included Howard Caygill,
Keri Davies, Ariel Hessayon, Arthur Versluis, amongst
others, with papers presented on a broad range of
topics from Blake's reading of Swedenborg to his influence on Georges Bataille and French literature. [1]

Iain's lecture, opening the proceedings and informally entitled 'Blake's London', lasted for approximately fifty minutes and spoke of Blake's unique sense of topography, both poetic and geographic, and the manner by which language and imagination conjoin to delineate a profound engagement with place. The lecture was warmly received. At the end questions were invited from the auditorium—packed with academics, students, Swedenborgians and Blake scholars alike—on topics both literary and personal.

The text printed here has undergone minor revision and endnotes have been added. References to Blake's poetry are to *Blake: Complete Works* edited by Geoffrey Keynes and citations are given in italics. Readers looking for corresponding themes in Iain's larger works should follow the references to *Hackney, That Rose-Red Empire,* his *London: City of Disappearances* and his most recent book *Ghost Milk: Calling Time on the Grand Project.*

Stephen McNeilly

Blake's London:
the topographic sublime

I 'm going to talk about William Blake and about what I decided to call, yesterday, on rereading elements of Blake, the 'topographic sublime'. A decision that was certainly countered by my walk here this morning from Hackney, the topographic ridiculous.

There is, over the forty-year period in which I've been living in the same place, a love of the fabric of this multidimensional city and also a cynical despair at the changes now being wrought. (It is interesting to think of them in terms of Blake.) New enclosures, blue fences and razor wire topped with surveillance cameras, have sealed off enormous tracts of terrain along the eastern

margin. We see the dominance of the virtual
over the actual, the computer-generated version
over the particulars of locality. You could see
this process as a perversion of Blake: conjuring
a deranged cosmology out of the future perfect
tense, through the corruption of language. The
anti-poetry of bureaucratic copywriters playing
with vacuous propaganda and warped sentiment.
Hackney Council opened up a swimming pool, but
you weren't allowed to take photographs. You can't
carry cameras inside the new Olympic Park, only
approved laptop imagery is sponsored. What you
are creating, in effect, is an electronic Golgonooza.
A system predicated on affectless gazing. Therefore
Los stands in London building Golgonooza,

Compelling his Spectre to labours mighty;
trembling in fear / The Spectre weeps, but
Los unmov'd by tears or threats remains.
"I must Create a System or be enslav'd
by another Man's. / "I will not Reason &
Compare: my business is to Create." [1]

How would these grand-project enclosures offend the libertarian spirit of someone like Blake? The city is being remade in the most dramatic and absolutist way since the original age of the railways, or the Blitz; landscapes that have lain dormant for many years, sometimes being nudged and revised, are now undergoing this troubling process, a lot of fence work, fence art. And weary crocodiles of the expelled are visible as ghosts on CCTV monitors: allotment holders, travellers, workers in inconvenient industries, artists in edgeland warehouses. High blue fences enclose things you must not look at. But at the same time, subversive art grows up to put pictures and slogans on old brick and new plywood. The hieratic head of Alfred Hitchcock, the voyeur's voyeur, appears as a transfer alongside Situationist quotations and, in several cases, lines from Blake. 'Human Thought is crush'd beneath the iron hand of Power.' There's now a fascinating interzone where a guerrilla street artist like the character known as Banksy is collected and patronized by Hollywood stars. Stencils and

strategic cartoons are either destroyed as acts
of public vandalism or endorsed by changing
hands for huge amounts of money. And you have
to argue over the fabric of the city as to whether
this is art the authorities want to sponsor (as they
have done in St Leonards-on-Sea, by immediate-
ly sealing a Banksy spray job under perspex); or
whether, in some mysterious way, these interven-
tions should remain an encrypted secret. We live
in a society avid for gathering up anything that
seems to have *spirit*; anything that is *danger-
ous* can be captured and converted into a form
of energy. Which is also wealth, money, credit,
sexual fulfilment.

Those are the images and thoughts that are
at the back of my mind when I invoke Blake,
and step out into the world, clutching the 1971
paperback I still turn to as a personal *I Ching*,
an almanac of divination. *Blake: Complete
Writings*. Edited by Geoffrey Keynes. Along with S
Foster Damon's *A Blake Dictionary*. And there's
another thing: the city as a hallucination. Just

walking here along the canal bank this morning,
I walked through clouds of cannabis smoke, I
walked through clouds of skunk, I walked past
early-breakfast drinking-discussion groups,
self-elected radicals and libertarians sitting on
benches with blue cans of Fosters lager. By the
time I had advanced two or three miles down
the canal bank, I was staggering, everything was
getting a little soft at the edges.

It reminded me of the writer Sarah Wise, a
notable London historian who has come up
with stories, and interrogated the legends, of
places that have disappeared from the official
surveys of the city. In a book I recently edited
called *London: City of Disappearances*, Sarah
provided a very useful gazetteer of vanishings
and deletions. She also wrote an account of
a series of murders undertaken by the resurrectionists who lived at Columbia Market, at
the edge of Hackney Road. And these people, in
the 1820s—a period when Blake is moving to
Fountain Court and when the peasant poet John

Clare visits London (both of these things we'll
return to)——were sweeping up street children
and vagrants and killing them by dosing them
with laudanum and porter, drowning them in
a well, and taking the bodies to sell to hospitals
for anatomy lectures. And the wives were taking
the clothes of these unfortunate victims around
street markets and peddling them. What emerges
most powerfully from Sarah's account is the
fact that the people committing the murders are
completely drunk. As soon as they've put the
violated corpses into the well, they go off to the
pub and they spend the night there. Then, the next
day, they make a series of hobbled progressions,
stopping and starting, wetting their whistles, across
London. So here we come back to topography,
and how you negotiate the city, how you choose
to remember the distinct zones, corner by corner,
building to building. The resurrectionists cross the
city, going from pub to pub to pub with a hand-
cart, a naked body in it to take to the hospital,
at Guy's or St Thomas', to sell to porters who are

themselves drunk, and who pass the specimen on to surgeons who are swilling claret upstairs. When the lowlife are caught, they are tried by judges who have to be propped up at the bench, black caps sliding from sweating, dripping heads. This is the London of Hogarth. The whole seething labyrinth is a hallucination of alcohol, pipe smoke, fumes. The only way to survive the squalor, the poverty, the degradation, is either to go into this fug of otherness, or, to cultivate that visionary sense. Clarity. Independence. Opposition. Everything that is in William Blake. That's where I begin.

I think of Blake more than anything else as a presence, a guide, an advocate. And the way I would come to him is that I would think . . . take Shakespeare, there's a book just published by Charles Nicholl, *The Lodger*, which has a very good account of Shakespeare living in a house in Cripplegate, a street that is no longer there. You've got an image of the man Shakespeare in London, but there isn't much in his work that is *specific* to London, beyond the comedy of

the picaresque, the borrowed dignity of heritage
settings. He lived in London, he worked in
London, he got his living in London. He drew
on the spirits of London, the pubs, churches,
brothels, palaces, and so on. But he doesn't
leave the imprint that Blake does. Blake actually
names areas and old villages and relishes ways of
moving through them, enormous cartographies
of absence and possession. The topography of
London becomes a kind of spiritual body and
almost a physical body for him. The descriptions
of Blake, from childhood, are of walking out,
pushing out from the centre—because he is born
at the centre, in Soho—moving into the folds of
the surrounding hills. The hills to the south tend
to be associated with visionary experience, trees
of angels in Peckham Rye. The trips to the north
were always painful. He writes, near the end of his
life, to John Linnell, saying:

*For I am again laid up by a cold in my
stomach. The Hampstead air, as it always*

did [...] When I was young, Hampstead,
Highgate, Hornsey, Muswell Hill, and even
Islington, and all places north of London,
always laid me up the day after, and some-
times two or three days, with precisely the
same complaint, and the same torment of
the stomach [...] [2]

So the landscape of London physically affects
him and it becomes part of him. And that was
the sense that I got from the very start of my
engagement with Blake and his prophetic books.

I came to London, to Brixton initially, in the
early 1960s, to attend film school and to train
as a documentary filmmaker. And then, after
having been to university in Dublin for four
years, I came back once again to London, where
I spent the rest of my life. My first impression,
on that return in 1967, was of a particular
point in our culture when Blake was being
recognized as a significant figure. That 1960s
counterculture found qualities in Blake to which

they instinctively responded. They re-invented him in their own image. He was pressed into the charivari of the *International Times* alongside William Burroughs, Wilhelm Reich and Michael Moorcock's Jerry Cornelius. This was not the topographer Blake. This was 'Glad Day'. Blake as celebrated by English poets like Michael Horovitz—and beyond that, beyond the confines of Notting Hill, by Allen Ginsberg, who stated repeatedly that he owed his core vision to the voice of the Lambeth poet.

In July 1967 I made a film with Ginsberg, at the time of the Congress of the Dialectics of Liberation in the Roundhouse, a film called *Ah! Sunflower.* And he said to me, and to anybody else who would listen, that his life was changed by the experience of being in a tenement flat in New York, at a moment when his friends and lovers, Neal Cassady, Jack Kerouac, Burroughs, had travelled to the west, and he was left on his own. He was reading Blake and, as he reads 'Ah! Sunflower', he hears this grave prophetic voice:

Ah, Sunflower! weary of time,
Who countest the steps of the sun,
Seeking after that sweet golden clime,
Where the traveller's journey is done— [3]

When I was filming Ginsberg, the place that he
wanted to visit was the top of Primrose Hill. And
we went to the top of Primrose Hill. We filmed
interviews with him there, and he read poems.
He had a red silken shirt with symbolic designs
painted by Paul McCartney—and we felt, as we
set up the camera, that Ginsberg was trying to
raise the spirit of Blake over the city again from
this vantage point. He spoke a lot about a poem
that George Barker had written, the poet of the
'40s associated with Dylan Thomas and David
Gascoyne. The poem was called *Calamiterror*; a
poem in which Blake appears in a vision over the
river Thames.

I saw William Blake large and bright like
ambition, / Absolute, glittering, actual

*and gold. / I saw he had worlds and
worlds in his abdomen, / And his bosom
innumerably enpeopled with all birds.
/ I saw his soul like a cinema in each of
his eyes, / And Swedenborg labouring
like a dream in his stomach.* [4]

So we have now, for the first time, the fusing
of Blake and Swedenborg, Blake and Ginsberg,
Blake and a genealogy of visionary English poets.
A fusion associated with sacred places: Thames,
Primrose Hill, Stonehenge. Swedenborg step-
ping ashore after that first voyage. Swedenborg
plunging, according to legend, naked into the
Fleet. His soul 'like a cinema' offering posthumous
visions to future supplicants, a potent ingredient
in London's dreaming. Ginsberg met another
poet called Harry Fainlight, now dead, on top of
Primrose Hill, and they sat down together with
their notebooks open, discussing Blake. And also
discussing the notion of Primrose Hill as being
somewhere of great spiritual significance.

Crabb Robinson, the diarist, talked to Blake, and Blake said to him, 'You never saw the spiritual Sun? I have. I saw him on Primrose Hill'. [5] And Blake writes of Primrose Hill: 'Primrose Hill is the mouth of [Los's] Furnace & the Iron Door'. [6] A more recent poet, Aidan Andrew Dun, who has written a visionary poem called *Vale Royal*, recapturing this spirit, set around King's Cross and St Pancras Old Church, drew on Blake's lines:

The fields from Islington to Marybone,
To Primrose Hill and Saint Johns Wood:
Were builded over with pillars of gold,
And there Jerusalems pillars stood. [7]

So the creation of a visionary city, a fourfold city, the London that is beneath and above temporal London, refers back to Blake. As well, later, to Rimbaud, who lived near this area and who undertook questing walks with Verlaine along the docks and rivers, before spending time researching in the British Museum, in the same way that, later still, Yeats was there revising and editing Blake.

That's where it started for me, the '60s sense of Blake, the sense of privileged topography. And Ginsberg goes away from the filming, as I discovered later, after we'd been on Primrose Hill, and away from his sense of this fabulous spread of London, looking towards those southern hills I talked about in relation to Blake's own expeditions. Ginsberg went to Wales, to the border country, and he wrote a poem called *Wales - A Visitation*, which was a totally Blakean project, a sense of Edenic Britain, with swathes of cloud, and he climbs through the mountains, and he tries to capture a bardic voice. And of course it's clear now that he was recalling Primrose Hill, the filming, the Post Office Tower, urban paranoia countered by the chorus of poets drawing on Blake.

Remember your day 150 miles from
London's / Symmetrical throned Tower

& network / of TV pictures flashing
bearded your Self. / Link the lambs of
the tree-nooked hillside of / This day with
the cry of Blake [...] [8]

Well, that was all very charming, a romantic
thing of youth, and worth referencing now,
youth has its virtues, but my reading had not
gone particularly deep and I hadn't made a real
connection with Blake in terms of my own life
and practice until I acquired this battered red
book, [9] on 23rd April 1971, from Compendium
Bookshop in Camden Town. Compendium was
the fountainhead bookshop of this era. It was
an independent bookshop that imported a lot of
stuff from America and Europe. At one time it
expanded so successfully that there was one shop
entirely filled with books of a spiritual nature, as
well as eco-politics, Gary Snyder. Another whole
shop full of poetry. I thought: 'This is a great
moment, things are really happening here'. Later
I found out that all this activity, the expansion

sitting with the mushrooming of Camden Market, was actually underwritten by drug money. A successful business plan. For a time. But you take what you get, and that shop was very important, and I got my Blake. I soon came upon a sequence that would affect the rest of my life and all the writing I did. It was *Jerusalem, The Emanation of the Giant Albion*. Which was, in a literal and metaphorical sense, where I lived: Albion Drive E8. And where I began publishing poetry in micro-editions. Mona Wilson, in her excellent biography of Blake, talks about the impossibility of reading the prophetic books, there is no audience for it, it's too complex, too crazy, you must start with *The Songs of Innocence* and so on . . . But *Jerusalem* was where I started. The sequence that I come back to time and time again goes:

> *He came down from Highgate thro'*
> *Hackney & Holloway towards London /*
> *Till he came to old Stratford & thence to*
> *Stepney & the Isle / Of Leutha's Dogs, thence*

*thro' the narrows of the River's side, / And
saw every minute particular: the jewels
of Albion, running down / The kennels of
the streets & lanes as if they were abhorr'd.
[...] / A building of Luvah, builded in
Jerusalem's eastern gate, to be / His
secluded Court: thence to Bethlehem where
was builded / Dens of despair in the house
of bread, enquiring in vain / Of stones
and rocks, he took his way, for human
form was none; / And thus he spoke,
looking on Albion's City with many tears* [10]

So here was a very interesting series of instruc-
tions, a particular kind of walk, and quite an
eccentric journey laid out, a trajectory which is
both spiritual and physical, and which suggests
that the eastern portion of the city, at that time,
was pretty much somnolent and well off the
official charts. If it was London, London had not
yet claimed it. Mills would give way to foul industries. Blake's lines spike the energy points, the

place names, and make London into a stripped
body. The litany of his mental journey is like
acupuncture.

I had been working as a gardener in
Limehouse, and I was cutting the grass of
Hawksmoor churches, which were then dirty,
grubby and spurned. Vagrants and drinking
schools were camped out around the Portland
stone recesses like medieval pilgrims or penitents
seeking sanctuary and a dole of British sherry,
the whole of Docklands, the Isle of Dogs, had
failed. The zone was derelict. Thatcherite
imperatives would not kick in for quite some
time yet. Capital didn't return to the river until
the Heathrow bullion blaggers needed territory
in which to invest. So what was the presence of
the eastern city? Well, Blake seemed to suggest
that it was a figure, a sleeping giant. He imagined
a figure of *inward*, an inward being. This self-
forged daemon belonged, I felt, to the ground of
London. It stood against the other great project
influencing me at that time, the mythopeic

structure cast by the American poet Charles Olson
in Gloucester, Massachusetts. Olson's epic, *The
Maximus Poems*, is dedicated to Robert Creeley
as the figure of *outward*. Olson projects his
odyssey as a journey through the local into the
star field, going out with the tide, understanding
the logistics of fishing fleets, understanding the
topography that lay *under* the ocean—the
mountain ranges of the Atlantic—and this push
becomes a reaching into the cosmos. Launched
with the minute particulars of place Blake talks
about, Olson's second movement carries you right
back, a return to the human nest. The particulars
have become myth. Blake, of course, is able to
do both of these things at once, the outward and
the inward. And for some reason the creation
of buildings and structures on the east side of
London seemed, prophetically, to suggest a new
kind of writing and even a new kind of social,
cultural, even biological, development.

Commentators at the time, writing about
Blake's *Jerusalem* itinerary, said 'Why Highgate?'

And the reason John Adlard put forward was that Highgate was then on the Great North Road—a road which subsequently moved east and up Stoke Newington and out through Tottenham. But, originally, it came over Highgate Hill—it was the great entrance to the city, even though Blake himself says, repeatedly, that he is uncomfortable in this landscape. Highgate is also connected to various forms of belief in Druidic sites. There were books like *Prehistoric London: Its Mounds and Circles*, written by Elizabeth Gordon before the First War, that suggested there were triangulations of energy across London, there were paths between important loci on Parliament Hill (with a tumulus), the Penton Mound in Islington, and the Tot Hill in Westminster. A projected triangle enclosing so many of the ancient energy generators of London. And Blake seems to have prefigured a lot of that too, but in a higher register. Curiously enough, there's this curvature, a swerving away: 'Highgate thro Hackney & Holloway towards London / Till he came to old

Stratford'. Well, this was the sticking point for people who wanted to discuss that journey: 'old Stratford', this was really peculiar. Adlard suggests, looking at texts of the time, that Blake actually meant 'old Ford', which was a point on the river Lea where Saxon and Viking England divided. A very important crossing point on the Lea and not further east to Stratford. But, uncannily, old Stratford is now the epicentre of everything, it is the new city, the virtual city growing up around the Olympic Park, the enclosed city with this huge blue fence around it. A city, symbolized by an Australian super-mall, which has taken itself out of the landscape. You could persuade yourself that Blake anticipates, or suggests the terminology for, future movements throwing up heretical temples, retail parks, structures that have to be confronted, discussed and debated. And destroyed. 'An Abstract objecting power that Negatives every thing.'

And when I think of enclosures, I think of a project I did much later, which was to follow the walk the peasant poet John Clare, who had

been in an asylum in Epping Forest, made over
three and a half days—forgive me for jump-
ing around, but this is a process of uncurling a
spiral, the twisted spine of a journey. John Clare
was in an asylum run by a man called Matthew
Allen in Epping Forest, on the fringes of London.
He had come to London down the Great North
Road, from his own village, Helpston, a little to
the north of Peterborough. There had been a
vogue for peasant poets, his poems were selling,
initially, in a way that Blake's never would. They
had gone through several editions. But this man,
the transported field labourer, had grown up in a
very enclosed society. The village was like an eye
that watched you all the way round, a pastoral
panopticon. And if he went beyond these safe
limits, as he did once, as a child, he described
it as going out of his knowledge: 'I didn't know
who I was because the birds, the stones, the
beasts, the insects no longer knew me. Therefore
I was nobody'. When he stayed within the area,
where he knew everything, he was also known.

So, coming to London was an enormous wrench and the journey was a small epic: to walk from Helpston to Stamford—six or seven miles early in the morning—then get the coach, an all-day ride, shaken, tumbled, exposed, to arrive in the dark, in London, and not know where you are. But, where he is, and this has never really been commented on, is right alongside where William Blake is. He goes to stay on the Strand, exactly where Blake has just moved into, leaving South Molton Street:

William Blake's landlord in South Molton Street sold his business in the spring of 1820. The Blakes, William and Catherine, decamped—books, pictures, sheets, port-folios, tools—to Fountain Court. Their final marital home was hidden away at the back of the Fountain tavern in the Strand. Close to the river. Strange to think of the two poets in such close proximity. William Blake wandering out to collect his jug of evening porter. And Clare, famously thirsty, shaking off his well-meaning minders. It didn't happen. Not in the only version of Clare's biography that we can assemble from accounts left by scholars and documented witnesses.

Writers are too deeply mired in fantasy to notice one another (except as rivals, caricatures, refractions of their own brilliance). Heads down, necks twisted: mud and stars. Two poets, in fortuitous conjunction, navigate trajectories through different cities that happen, just then, to be in one place. They are blind as comets. [11]

They have no sense of each other.

Clare, before he left Helpston, had been out in the fields on one of his walks. He was attempting, as was his practice, to get away from the eyes of the village, to find a place where he could write. And he saw three men in the fields with sticks and chains doing something that he thought to

be a magical ritual, a ceremony. And they were
surveyors for the railway. And once the railway
had come——a great ladder out of London,
clawing this place in——it was over. This village
had been absorbed into another totality, into the
shadows of London. Did this event initiate the split
in Clare's mind? He couldn't be in two places. He
couldn't be in either of them. In London, he's lost.
In Fleet Street, where he goes to visit his publisher,
to Taylor's offices, he just sits in the window for
hours, watching the passing streams of people.
Blake is supposed to walk endlessly in London——
he knows what he's doing. Clare doesn't. He
doesn't know how the city works. He knows how to
walk in the country. So, he's marooned there, fixed
on a window ledge. The other thing that destroys
him is the agricultural enclosures that happen
in the English landscape. Suddenly this village,
all the common ground, is divided up into an
eccentric jigsaw of little parcels. He can no longer
walk, he fears to walk in the fields for the farmers
turning him off. And the only times he finds work,

it is as a hedger. Suddenly he doesn't understand his own landscape. Which is also his language.

When enclosures came to London, to Hackney for example, on Hackney Downs, a patch of common ground was fenced in, ancient liberties suspended. The mob, the Londoners, wouldn't accept it. They tore down the fences and they stripped the crop, and they took it away as their own because they demanded this land as their birthright. Where we are now, in Blake's old Stratford, without consultation, overnight, a high blue fence encloses common land, marshland, lammas land, a place for walking free. The allotments that were there, Manor Garden Allotments, all of that was torn down. My initial impression is of Blake as a red-cap libertarian in the crowd at the burning of Newgate Prison. At that period of his life, he's a firebrand, an enthusiast of revolutions. Politics and mysticism, craft and art, vanity and modesty: they struggle. And the fight within himself——and the deep argument with what he knows of Swedenborg——is conducted through a reconfiguring of the topography of London. That which he will permit to be enclosed, wrapped in skin and sinew, and that which will break forth as chant or song or image. Sexual imperatives, chains of poverty and oppression. Entry to the world of dreams and visions.

There's another way of seeing Blake as a Londoner, which is something like the version promoted by Peter Ackroyd's *Blake*. This is a persuasive account of the poet's life, a chronological narrative: where he lived and how the books were written. But there's a process in there that involves risky leaps of imagination. A heritaged version of what Blake might, and perhaps should, have been. Ackroyd talks about Hercules Road where the Blakes lived, in Lambeth, south of the river:

> *From his upstairs window, Blake would have seen the wherries and fishing boats and sailing ships upon the Thames, where the riverbank had, over the*

centuries, become the site of coal wharfs and timber yards. [12]

Well, I don't know. I, in the course of things, have walked these streets and visited all the sites where Blake lived. But, you can't get it by that method, you can't reach back in any way. Hercules Road is a reef of blanked and impenetrable public housing, a run-down pub (or it was at that time), and there's no way that you sustain any sense of the river, which is some distance back from the road. You do get a sense of the asylum near there, Bedlam, the Bethlehem Hospital, which had moved across from Moorfields in 1815 ——in the way that London always wants to earth or dispose of its visionary madness, its damaged citizens. If you wanted to understand where London finished as an organic entity, you would walk out until you hit the necklace of lunatic asylums.

When I was navigating a path around the M25 on foot—this orbital motorway that goes around London—I found that it was defined

by Victorian and Edwardian parks, containing
hospitals and asylums, all of which have now
been decommissioned and turned into gated
communities, luxury communities. But there
was this underlying feeling that those who were
difficult, mad, damaged, whatever, from the
centre, would be pushed out to the edge. Foucault
talks about that. It's partly a healing process
to take people into parkland where they will be
put to work in gardens, to work with animals.
And it's partly a removal of a malignancy that
might affect the rest of the city. Now, a lot of the
more cultured, socially successful people of the
era, the university poets, would have looked on
Blake, if they were interested in him at all, as
being one of the tribe of the mad. Charles Lamb,
who was quite positive and enthusiastic about
elements of Blake, did see him as a special case,
touched by genius, but *touched*, a madman. And
Blake himself would have been thrust out. The
journey to Felpham, down to the south coast,
where he finds himself possessed by the spirit

of Milton, is a removal of a sort. And it doesn't work. It becomes horrible in the end and there is no way but to come back to the city. The gravity of London draws him all the time. Where it is drawing him to is, in some sense, a place that is the great oasis for walkers or thinkers about London, which is Bunhill Fields, where the Lambeth visionary is buried in a multiple-occupation paupers' grave.

They have now moved the memorial to Blake, the stone with his name and that of Catherine carved on it, away from the earth in which they placed his bones. The triangulation of memorials in Bunhill Fields represents London's dissenting spirit. There's William Blake; and right next to him, Daniel Defoe; and opposite, on the other side of a paved path, John Bunyan. All three were topographers in their way. Bunyan, the tinker from Bedford, has the cartography of the actual journeys he has made as a walker transposed on a spiritual map, a journey through difficulty to the shining city on the hill. And Blake engages with this project of Bunyan's, and makes a series of drawings, recasting that pilgrimage. Whereas Defoe, who lived in Stoke Newington and who also operated a business down on the Thames Estuary, was more a man of affairs, an intelligencer. He adventures on a tour around the whole of Britain, but in a double identity. Partly as a recorder of what is going on socially—a freelance cultural historian, maker of documentaries. Partly as a reporter back—a spy. A double man.

The fascinating thing is to place these three people in this lovely zone. On a morning like this, it would be wonderful, with the trees overhead, the dappled leaves—there is a large fig tree that hangs over Blake's grave. And it's a place that is *not* in the City. It's just outside the walls of the original City. Because once you go beyond, the permissions begin to open up. The original theatres grew up just on the edge of the City. The brothels, the liberties, the asylums grew up in Hoxton, on the edge, and in Hackney, because they're the suburbs of the City. And in

this place too the dissenters are buried. And I go
through that place and sit down because it is
a relief from any journey across town——in the
same way Blake has laid out his trajectory down
from Highgate, starting at the hill. Down, even
though it is a painful thing for him in lots of
ways, it disturbs him to be out there, even men-
tally. The place on the edge of the City is a place
of respite and resolution. I visited it quite recently, just before *City of Disappearances* came out,
because I'd heard that the lost grave of William
Blake had been found:

> *The keeper, the Irishman, was unusual.*
> *He was there when you needed him, but*
> *he was otherwise invisible. When Bunhill*
> *Fields was a subject, this man was always*
> *mentioned by initiates. Some said he was*
> *an artist, a painter. They didn't know his*
> *name, had never set eyes on his work.*
> *There was a distance, certainly, between*
> *the person who stood, so obligingly, before*

you, and whoever came, by accident or whim, to the old Nonconformist burial ground on the edge of the City. The unlucky Cromwells, he had those on tap. He would unlock a low gate and lead you to the relevant memorial, the chipped or erased tomb. He had stories, without the compulsion to inflict them on you. And he did his job, quietly and efficiently: the gardening, sweeping, toilet cleaning. The brewing of regular mugs of tea.

A slight figure in a baseball cap and overalls, you may have noticed him ghosting through television films, local interest documentaries. The man solved one of the mysteries of the place. Who, I wanted to know, left flowers on the grave of William and Catherine Blake? There was no such tribute for Daniel Defoe or John Bunyan. Pass through as early as you like, they were there, in a jam jar; fresh, modest. A splash of colour against the grey. 'That's me', he confessed. But I think the coins which have recently made an appearance are not *him. Brown. Leaving a stain when they are lifted—so that the new tributes can be placed, next morning, in exactly the same position. Three groups of coins on the rim of the thick slab: five at each end and seven on the highest part, the curve. I'd have made something of that once.*

The keeper rubbed his nose with a knuckle and confirmed what I'd read in The Times *(16 April 2005), Blake wasn't here. The much-loved memorial was just that, a prompt marking nothing, marking absence. Two 'amateur sleuths' —Carol Garrido, a landscape gardener, and her husband, Luis, a law graduate —'had used records from* Bunhill Fields Burial Ground Order Book *to find the grave's coordinates'.*

The present memorial had been set up in 1960, an episode of civic pride, to smooth over minor bomb damage, after the Blitz. Fading newspaper photographs of the moustache-and-black-hat dignitaries, taped to the window of the keeper's hut, made it absolutely clear: the dedication ceremony happened elsewhere.

We looked at mute grass and away to the west, beyond the line of the trees, to the obelisk of St Luke's, Old Street. Not a trace. Not one degree of the original heat. A communal grave: even in death, a shared tenement for the Lambeth poet. I read out the list of names, co-tenants of this Clerkenwell pit: Margaret Jones, 37; Rees Thomas, 53; Edward Sherwood, 53; William Blake, 69; Mary Hilton, 62; James Greenfield, 38; Magdalen Colin, 81, of Bethnal Green Road; and Rose Davis, 58.

The Necropolis Company took a million-pound contract to clear the slumbering dead, in strong green bags, from beneath St Luke's. Winter rains turned

*earth to muddy soup. Kosovans were
employed—willing active workers—to
feel, blind, for bones, scraps of cloth,
coffin wood. And then the logged remains,
details entered in an antique ledger,
were taken out to the suburbs and bull-
dozed into a mass grave. Which was soon
re-turfed and rolled.*

*'They're everywhere', said the man who
made the film. 'London is a great mound
of bones. We are walking on the faces of
the dead'. Before Brookwood, the funeral
trains out of Waterloo, and the subur-
banization of death, our immediate
forefathers were much closer to the surface. Hands reached out of the ground,
literally. Hoxton urchins were challenged
for wearing small fists of signet rings.
Respectable matrons, walking nervously
through churchyards, skidded on human
skin, mortality's leather.*

Blake was put to earth with a charabanc

of East Enders, recent immigrants from
the Celtic fringe. No alcove in St Paul's,
no effigy in a winding sheet. No heritage
plaque (like a royal blue satellite dish),
not then. And better so. Beyond the reach
of vulgar curiosity. A stone postcard in the
shade of a fig tree. And the company of
other distinguished absentees. All under
the patronage, the casual and affectionate
custodianship, of this Irishman, my guide.
His daily jam jar of garage flowers. [13]

There is an interesting book by Gerda Norvig, a
closely worked account of Blake's illustrations to
The Pilgrim's Progress. From my point of view,
the intriguing thing was that this book became a
touchstone for a painter called Renchi Bicknell,
who had lived in Hackney in the communal
house to which I had moved in 1968 (the period
I previously mentioned, when Blake was such
an influence). Renchi, in the following decades,
pushed further and further west, but he returned to

join me on our peregrination around London——
London Orbital——when we walked the length
of the M25, through what is called the acoustic
footprints, to try and recover a sense of where the
sprawling metropolis started and where it gave up
its ghosts. Having completed that project, he then
accompanies me on a walk from Epping Forest,
retracing John Clare's steps, when the troubled
poet escaped from Matthew Allen's asylum and
trudged all the way home, in the expectation of
reuniting with his childhood sweetheart, Mary
Joyce——who was in fact dead, who had died,
from the after-effects of burns, while he was in
the asylum. Arriving on the fringes of Peterborough, Clare is met by his actual wife, Patty, and
a cart sent out to fetch him. He doesn't recognize
her, and is hauled aboard, brought to the new
cottage, 'tried' and found wanting. And in this
brief period of months that he spent at home, he
writes a wonderful account, a letter describing
this journey, his flight. And to trace that letter——because there are questions of academic

copyright with Clare's material—the only way was to actually go to the library in Northampton and be given the original journal to look at, and to make my own accurate transcription.

And in doing so, I was reminded very much of the lines of Blake I quoted of the walk down from Highgate, because how it appears in the book is quite different from how it appears in the facsimile editions of Blake's own plates. The punctuation on this page of Blake does not bother with apostrophes. The page is like a block of red rain. It is wonderfully encoded, like a Mayan codex, rather than the Geoffrey Keynes version, 'corrected' to a more formal grammar. In the rush and spirit of it, engraved by Blake, the journey becomes one enormous charge, and that is exciting to see. And the figures at the bottom of the plate . . . there is a naked figure with a shell-like head—and that's what I thought I recovered from Hercules Road when I went there. There was no sense that you could re-imagine the poet looking out of his upstairs window and

seeing the boats on the Thames. I was inspecting
the dirt on the ground, the sand of a builder's
tip, and in it was this shining shell. It could have
been the fragment of a snail shell or a seashell
of some sort, there was just this one little white
shard. I picked it up, I couldn't resist it. And it
seemed to be, I don't know, a retrieval of a glittering particular, a detail, a clue, that in some way,
maybe sentimentally, led me back into a notion
of what I got from Blake *as a presence*. As this
ultimate guide and presence in the city.

Renchi, who'd completed the walks with me,
completed both walks, M25 and John Clare's
Journey out of Essex, then got hold of Norvig's
book about Blake's versions of Bunyan and
The Pilgrim's Progress, and he taught himself
etching and began a project of his own: to
recreate, or reconsecrate, a version of the walks
and journeys that he'd taken, epic ones all across
England, combined with a reading of Norvig's
text. In a self-published booklet, *A Pilgrim's
Progress*, he pays his dues to his mentors:

The initial inspiration for this series came from my purchase and devouring of Dark Figures in the Desired Country *by Gerda S. Norvig. This has been my bible and like Blake's version of Christian (Plate II), reading his book, I have buried my head in it intently* [...]

Learning from William Blake, while I transposed his line and wash drawings into etchings, I was always in awe and wonder of his VISION—and his skill in extracting the Archetypal material from John Bunyan's original text—then bringing it alive through its 28 iconic stages into sustained VISION. [14]

So the process goes on and on. So we're sucked into the vortex of energy, in the way that I was sucked into seeing landscape through Blake, or seeing it through the connections between the Hawksmoor churches. That old London, as you looked at it, was a forest of steeples of

churches. It was like looking at the river itself,
as it had been full of craft, and you knew the city
through these stone fingers, pointing in spiritual
affirmation towards the sky. And everyone in
London *belonged* to one of these zones. You were
fined, as Shakespeare was, if you failed to attend
your nominated local church. So the whole
map of energy was different. And acoustically it
was different too, each of these churches made
particular noises, bells were rung competitively.
And the smells would also have located you, the
meat, the dung, the sweat. The crafts associated
with certain streets and courts. That's gone. We
don't have that way of reading things anymore.
The pushing through of the railways, the cutting
of canals, the construction of virtual cities, all
of this affects and remakes the topography of
London. But you can get back. Time comes in
layers, it's plural, where place is singular. You
can get back to De Quincey. You can go back to
Blake. You can go back to Blake meditating on
The Pilgrim's Progress.

Gerda Norvig sees this image of Christian with his burden as a form of entrapment. A man peering short-sightedly at the book is himself captured within the pages of another book, at which we, the tentative readers, also peer. The gaze is not easily broken. Bunyan's carapace disintegrates, a memento to the passage of time. But the panel with the pilgrim is fresh and bright, the author's death dream is realized and framed. A storm is brewing, Norvig tells us, the man is bent double with wakeful pain and anguish, he wears ragged trousers and a torn shirt, and his limbs show extreme muscular exertion as if he were straining upwards against the equal and opposite downward force of his burden. There is no escape. We have come to a place that describes gloriously the place we have come to. So disappear into the image, the stone mirror, or stand here forever confirmed in your ignorance.

My first book that really engaged with this was called *Lud Heat*. Inspired by Blake, I had my own small press and was making my own books,

and the frontispiece of the original edition of
that book was this image, from *The Pilgrim's
Progress*, the figure bent double under this burden, which I saw as being a symbolic thing of the
journey, the quest——the difficulty of the journey, the necessity of the journey——and that for
the next whatever number of years, I would be
physically struggling across the landscape, under
the burden of greater writers, greater books,
previous memories, the noise and density of the
city. And this was true. Shortly after that, I was
marking out lines on Hackney Marshes, which
was a wonderful job. You started on Monday, you
whitewashed this geometry into this inspirational
landscape under the clouds, and it took you the
whole week, and then on Saturday and Sunday
everybody came and played football and kicked it
to pieces. And you started again the next Monday.
So it was eternal repetition. Constructing a pre-
Olympic virtual geometry out of lime and seeing
it erased in a couple of hours. A useful lesson.
Those football pitches, now trimmed to make car

parks for the Games, were built over the rubble of blitzed terraces. You have another lost London right under the grass.

And a book dealer, originally from Hackney, a rag trade person who wanted to become a publisher, and who published John Cowper Powys, a man called Jeff Kwintner, arrived in a blue Rolls Royce Corniche outside my house one night, as I came back from the Marshes, and took me on to work. This was his version of Blake: to reconfigure London and gather in all these strange marginal figures and employ them to produce books. The first thing he said to me was: 'Your karma is always to be carrying huge burdens across the city'. And it was true. I always had bags of books, camera equipment, children, whatever. Even today I've got a small burden, but the nice thing is, as you get older, the burden does get less, more and more of it is spilled out, and more and more is passed on to other people, and that's how it ends. And it is this image that is Gerda Norvig's onion peeled into Blake, extracted into Renchi Bicknell's engravings. The golden chain goes on and on and on, and the words of guidance, the maps we need to follow, are all to be found in the works of the archetypal London writer, William Blake of Lambeth.

Q&A

Q: *Listening to your descriptions of old London, very Hogarthian, and new London, which has been blue-fenced, there is an implication that the spirit of prophecy we see in Blake is yet to reach its full badness. What is your feeling about how bad things are?*

A: That's quite a difficult one and I'm wrestling with it at the moment. I'm writing a book that is wholly set within the boundaries of the sprawling borough where I live, a book called *Hackney, That Rose-Red Empire*. I was mentioning stories I'd heard from doctors who'd worked in hospitals. And throughout all this process——I must have done 60 or 80 interviews——the sense was just what you were talking about, a sense of loss, decline, community breaking up, significant buildings destroyed. We're in a wonderful place here, in the lecture theatre at Swedenborg House, and I'm told that the architect is also the architect of a synagogue in Hackney. These things shift and change. London is a perpetual argument between revision and stasis, what we elect to remember and what we are prepared to sacrifice. I've often talked of writers as the 're-forgotten'. The old villages of London are like that too.

There was a notable Victorian theatre in Dalston Lane. It began as a circus space, then became a music hall theatre, an immense, immense building. By the 1920s, it was revised into the most state-of-the-art, technologically up-to-the-moment cinema in London, and because it was relatively close to the railway, it became a cultural epicentre. And numerous people recalled grandparents meeting at one

of those venues, marrying, and their kids
going back when it later became a music club,
The Four Aces. Finally, it was a club called
Labyrinth, part of the rave culture. This building
had shifted and changed, made necessary
adjustments, right through the generations. It
had well-recorded internal details, architectural
elements, stairs, decorations. But the forces of
development, or whatever, partly as a result of
the Olympics, declared that what they described
as 'an enormous concrete shelf' had to be laid
down, so that the railway could be revamped.
And this building, rather dubiously, was pulled
down overnight. It disappeared, nothing, a field
of rubble, a blank, which was quite shocking.
But what was more shocking was that the people
doing it made a heritage pitch to say that what
they were doing was bringing back what was
there before—a connection with the railway.
But the fact is that, during the period I was
living there, that railway link to Liverpool Street
was stripped out. When I first lived there in the

'60s, you could take a train down to the City, it was a wonderful run. But that was removed, the railway was gone, and bringing it back becomes an excuse for destroying this fabric. What goes with it is the fact that people who did not want to move, or who lived in buildings like this, applied to English Heritage to have preservation orders. In numerous cases, fifteen or sixteen, the petitioners suffered fires, properties were arson attacked. The level of development muscle behind this vandalism is quite frightening. It's corporate, off-shore money. The deal is being done with invisible people and all respect for the local, the sense of local democracy, is gone.

So, I do feel, in answer to your question, a sense of loss and shame. But is this to do with being of a certain age, trying to cling on to images I like? There is a different world out there, undoubtedly. Electronic, connected. New communities, new technologies. And I don't think it is all going to be negative. I think it is apocalyptic in some senses, but what emerges is a different way of thinking,

a different way of behaving. Once upon a time,
if you'd come along the canal, there would have
been no one on it. Well, this morning, that canal
has become a bicycle track. It is difficult to walk
because there are hundreds and hundreds of
bicycles, a furious peloton. The kind of middle-
class, white, incoming, wealthier elements of the
area have transferred out of public transport.
The whole of public transport is a magnificent
multi-tongued babble of voices and fast-food
cuisines and people talking on phones, and
also introducing all kinds of interesting viruses.
Buses are like freelance ambulances or burger
vans. But the richer people don't use buses, they
go on bicycles, which is quite weird. You've got
very expensive bicycles, helmets, people seriously
slapping along. Walking zones are under threat,
permissions are suspended. The whole city is
changing and absorbing new influences at a
phenomenal rate. I think there will be positives as
well, but we're going to have to go through a very
difficult time in this interim period, and accept

that much has to be fought for, much has to be discussed in places like this. These are great spaces that still exist, but they are becoming secret and special, so this is why I am really honoured and pleased to come here today.

Q: *William Blake, in the hymn and poem,* Jerusalem, *and his general twinning of Jerusalem with Albion, seems to give [a sense of a] British Israelite poet, albeit an alternative one. Some of the other poets you mentioned seem to have that too. Ginsberg, coming here in the '60s, brought a Jewishness to bear on that Blakean Albion and, I think, helped in that process. Then, Harry Fainlight is Anglo-American Jewish as well, very much a Blakean spirit operating in all those areas. And even Aidan Andrew Dun is of Judaeo-Celtic origin and is continuing that project. And maybe that is good when Washington, London and Israel are engaged in other types of projects——these poets seem to offer a poetic antidote to that. I was just wondering what thoughts you have on this poetic British Israelite tradition?*

A: Well, I don't think I'd ever thought about it until you mentioned it just now. It's interesting. The other element you mentioned was Celtic. I grew up in South Wales and was educated in Ireland, so I had a feeling of coming into this territory from outside, in a slightly subversive Celtic way.

I'm thinking of something we discussed before the event started, we were talking about the head of Swedenborg. What haunts me is that Swedenborg was buried in a Swedish church in Wellclose Square, but the head disappeared at some point and went off on all kinds of adventures ... but there's a poem written by Vernon Watkins, who was a friend of Dylan Thomas, and a kind of Christian mystic poet who lived outside Swansea, called 'Swedenborg's Skull':

So I see it today, the inscrutable mask of

*conception / Arrested in death. Hard, slender
and grey, it transcends / The enquiring
senses, even as a shell toiling inward, /
Caught up from the waters of change by a
traveller who bends / His piercing scrutiny,
yields but a surface deception, / Still
guarding the peace it defends.*[15]

A generous, courteous man. I visited Watkins
in his bungalow on the Gower Peninsula, as a
schoolboy. And he listened to my probably man-
nerless and awkward questions with such respect
and answered with such seriousness. I'd forgotten,
in the Swedenborg poem, that 'shell'. Which now
reminds me of the fragment I picked up, outside
Blake's house in Hercules Road. Watkins even has
a traveller bending forward with 'piercing scrutiny'. Swedenborg complementing Blake, yet again,
more markers on the sacred topography.

Swedenborg's head had lodged in Swansea,
unnoticed and unremarked, until Watkins
wrote this. And that's my insight into this

culture, the links between London and Wales. We always thought of London, as it is depicted in mythological texts like the Mabinogion as a Welsh city, formed around the buried head of the giant Bran at Tower Hill. David Jones, who knew Watkins well, and corresponded with him, would be perhaps the ultimate Cockney-Celtic poet. But that's another digression. The figure of Bladud, who is an English Icarus, flies from Bath, a shaman, and crashes on Ludgate Hill, on the temple there that becomes St Paul's Cathedral. All of these things combine and interweave with that Jewish tradition you speak of, and both traditions respond very deeply to the figure of Blake, through his interest in the Kabbalah, his interest in Boehme and so on. He is the portal to so much of this. Maybe, in the end, we all find what we want in Blake, in the fat red book, it's such a rich loaf.

Q: *You mentioned the walk in east London that went to old Ford in Stratford. Is that where it stops or does it continue south of the river?*

A: That particular walk that Blake describes goes through 'the narrows of the Rivers side', and stops at the river. The 'Isle / Of Leutha's Dogs', he talks about. One of the very important things in this journey is that he never crosses the river within a sequence. There is a strong sense of what it is, being in Lambeth on the south shore, or describing these journeys on the north shore which don't cross the river, they finish up on the edge of the water. Who or what are 'Leutha's Dogs'? There's been some discussion about how going through 'the narrows of the Rivers side' was a reference to Narrow Street, in Limehouse. I think that's being a bit pedantic. But 'Leutha's Dogs', a lot of commentators believe, is a reference to levels of prostitution on the edge of the dockland area.

In Victoria Park there are two brick plinths with dog statues on, called the *Dogs of Alcibiades*. And every time they go up, they are vandalized. And with these smashed faces and missing limbs, they become symbolic—what a book dealer would call a 'dog' is a really ruined and terrible book—and these symbolic twin dogs seem to relate, once again, to that Blakean journey, as if the Isle of Dogs is an unlucky place. When Ben Jonson wrote his play, *The Isle of Dogs*, he was prosecuted, persecuted, jailed, and the play disappears, it doesn't exist. There is something dark and miasmic about this notion of the Isle of Dogs, where Blake's road map finishes up. He doesn't cross rivers.

I remember being with the great London writer, Michael Moorcock (who had grown up on the south side, in those hills, and had moved to west London), walking down to Westminster Bridge. I started off across the bridge, and I realized he'd gone! I came back and he's standing there and he says, 'I can't. I can never cross water, I can't go back there'. Everything, all the ghosts of childhood. Angela Carter, who lived not too far from the river in Wandwsworth, starts her final novel by saying that London is like Budapest, a city divided by the river. It's two cities. And I think that's true, in a kind of literal sense, and a spiritual sense. And so that's why that particular journey of Blake's never carries on, like our new Overground railway, and crosses to the south side.

Endnotes

1   Other speakers and topics at the conference were: Philip
    Broadhead, 'The Influence of Lutherans and Moravians
    on the Religious Life of Blake's London'; Howard
    Caygill, 'Blake and Science'; Keri Davies, 'Blake and
    the Moravians'; Ariel Hessayon, 'Blake and Radical
    Traditions'; Richard Lines, 'Blake, Swedenborg and
    Swedenborgians'; Stephen McNeilly, 'Blake and French
    Literature'; Robert Rix, 'Blake, Swedenborg and Animal
    Magnetism'; Michael Simpson, 'Blake and the Reading
    Nation'; Devin Zuber, 'Green London as the New
    Jerusalem: Swedenborg and Blake's Urban Ecology'; and
    Arthur Versluis, 'Blake's Place in the Esoteric Tradition'.

TEXT
1   William Blake, *Jerusalem*, plate 10, see *Blake:
    Complete Writings*, ed. Geoffrey Keynes (Oxford: Oxford
    University Press, 1966), p. 629.
2   Alexander Gilchrist, *Life of William Blake* (London:
    Macmillan and Co, 1863), vol. I, p. 347.

3 William Blake, 'Ah! Sunflower', see *Blake: Complete Writings*, p. 215.

4 George Barker, *Calamiterror* (London: Faber & Faber, 1937).

5 Quoted in Alexander Gilchrist, *The Life of William Blake*, p. 360.

6 Blake, *Jerusalem*, plate 73, l. 54, see *Blake: Complete Writings*, p. 714.

7 Ibid., plate 27, p. 649.

8 Allen Ginsberg, *Wales - A Visitation* (London: Cape Goliard Press, 1968).

9 *Blake: Complete Writings*, ed. Geoffrey Keynes.

10 William Blake, *Jerusalem*, plate 31, ll. 14-28, p. 657.

11 Iain Sinclair, *Edge of the Orison: In the Traces of John Clare's 'Journey out of Essex'* (London: Hamish Hamilton, 2005), p. 91

12 Peter Ackroyd, *Blake* (London: Sinclair-Stevenson, 1995).

13 Iain Sinclair, *London: City of Disappearances* (London: Hamish Hamilton, 2006), p. 187.

14 Renchi Bicknell, *A Pilgrim's Progress* (Glastonbury: Flying Dragon, 2008).

15 Vernon Watkins, *Cypress and Acacia* (London: Faber, 1959).